The Music in Derrick's Heart

The Music in Derrick's Heart

by Gwendolyn Battle-Lavert

illustrated by Colin Bootman

Holiday House / New York

The heat lay on Derrick's front porch like a wool coat. It didn't bother him. He was waiting for Uncle Booker T. The old man had promised to teach him the harmonica this summer.

All of a sudden Derrick saw a slim, dark man strutting down the road. His eyes flashed as dark as his patent-leather shoes. His head bobbed a bit from side to side. "Mama, he's coming!" shouted Derrick.

Mama called out, "Uncle Booker T., I'm sure glad you're here. You know Derrick. He holds you to a promise."

Uncle Booker T. said, "A promise is a promise. These old hands still got a few good songs left in them. Papa taught me well.

"Come on, son! We'll take a trip around the neighborhood. You can't be poking around. Summer ain't as long as it seems."

Derrick and Uncle Booker T. scampered away, away, away. They moved with rhythm in the street. Uncle Booker T. played gold and silver notes. Cheek to cheek. Face to face. Their noses testing the air. Twisting and turning. Turning and twisting. The music got in their hands and feet. They made a circle of the town.

As the sun was going down, they made it back to Derrick's front porch. Uncle Booker T. put his old harmonica in Derrick's hands. That's when the lessons began.

Derrick blew strange, wild notes.

Uncle Booker T. moaned, "Slow down! Don't rush! Tadpoles don't turn into frogs overnight. Papa told me, 'Booker T., music is something you hear with your ears. But you've got to feel it with your heart.' So slow down! Take your time. I'm going to let you keep this old harmonica every night."

Long after Uncle Booker T. was gone, Derrick practiced, practiced, practiced.

His mama called, "Derrick, put that harmonica away. It's time to go to sleep."

Derrick went to sleep with the harmonica clenched in his hand.

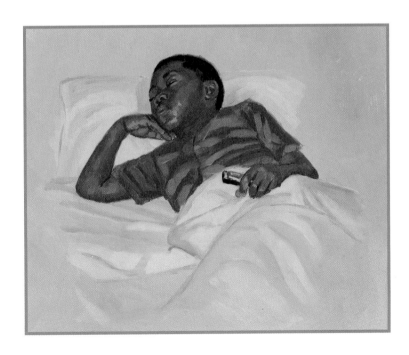

As the days grew hotter, Derrick's and Uncle Booker T.'s feet grew slower and slower. Sometimes they sat on Big Mama's front porch. She always had a big platter of homemade teacakes and a pitcher of squeezed lemonade.

"Booker T.," said Big Mama, "play my favorite hymn. I need a song to lift my spirits."

Uncle Booker T. closed his eyes. He put the harmonica to his lips. He concentrated so hard it hurt to watch him. Soft and slow. Slow and soft.

If there was a breeze, the big pecan trees in the yard surely blocked it. But Big Mama didn't care about the heat. She waved her weatherworn fingers through the steamy air. Every now and then she moaned in time with the beat. "Oh, glory! Hallelujah!"

"Big Mama," said Derrick. "Why you cry! Is Uncle Booker T.'s music hurting you?"

Big Mama clapped her hands together. "Lordy, no! Your uncle Booker T.'s songs just set my soul on fire," she said. "I'm thinking of all our kinfolk who have gone on to glory. If Booker T. keeps on playing like that, we going to have church right here."

Uncle Booker T. said, "I just play the songs I know."

That night after he practiced, Derrick slept with the harmonica taped to his heart.

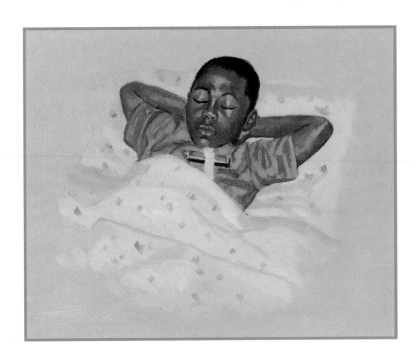

Some days Derrick sat on the stoop while Uncle Booker T. played his song. He said, "My song is a happy song. There ain't no words. Just sweet, sweet music."

Uncle Booker T. cocked his head to one side. You would have thought there was a wind the way his body swayed back and forth. When he finished, his hands were wet with sweat.

Afterward, the lessons continued. Uncle Booker T.'s skillful hands guided Derrick's across the harmonica.

Before bed, Derrick practiced. He slept with the harmonica on top of his head.

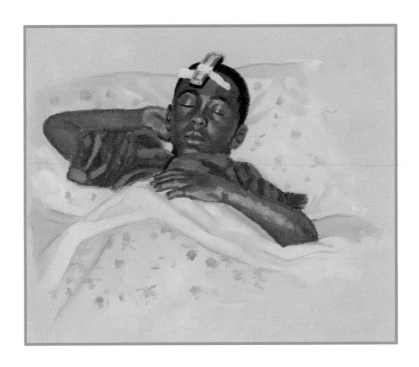

From sun up to sun down. From street to street. Twisting and turning. Turning and twisting. All day long, after every song, Derrick asked, "Uncle Booker T., do I have the feeling yet?"

Uncle Booker T. always replied, "Don't rush! Take your time."

On Mondays they went to Aunt Agnes's. It was her wash day. The white sheets on her clothesline snapped and popped in the noonday sun.

"Oh, Booker T.! You got to play me some jazz," said Aunt Agnes.

Uncle Booker T. started playing. Smooth and swinging. Short and choppy. Colorful notes that Uncle Booker T. dragged up and down the yard.

"Lord, I'd know that tune anywhere," said Aunt Agnes. "It don't come from nowhere but the heart. Come on, Derrick, let me show you how to swing."

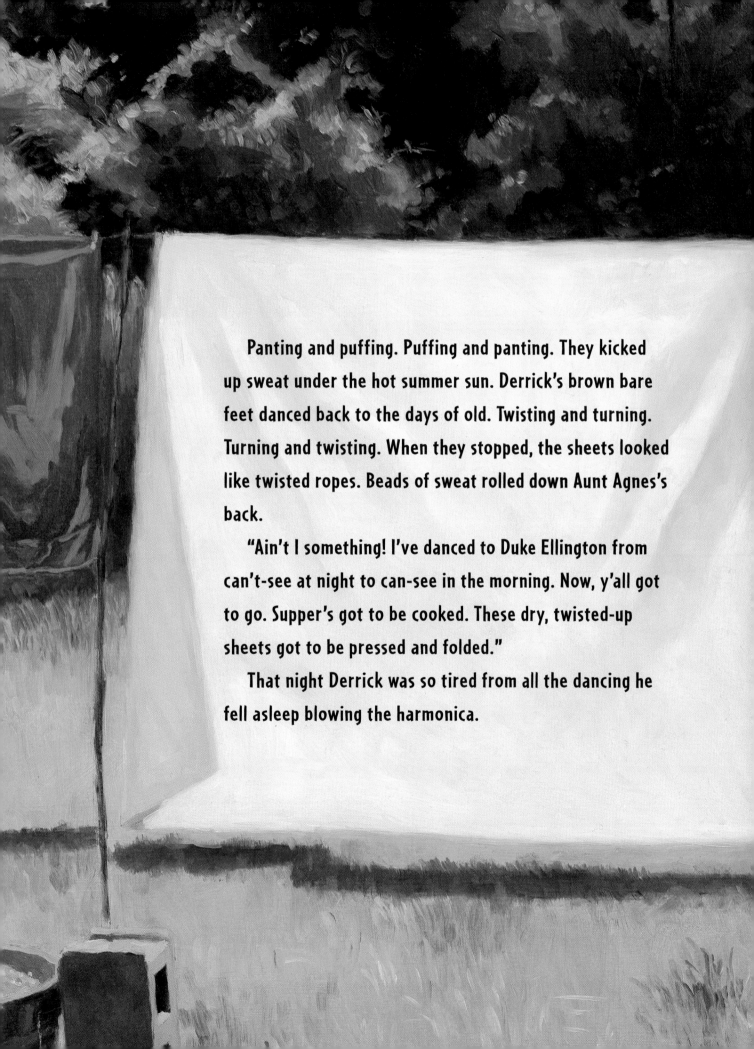

Panting and puffing. Puffing and panting. They kicked up sweat under the hot summer sun. Derrick's brown bare feet danced back to the days of old. Twisting and turning. Turning and twisting. When they stopped, the sheets looked like twisted ropes. Beads of sweat rolled down Aunt Agnes's back.

"Ain't I something! I've danced to Duke Ellington from can't-see at night to can-see in the morning. Now, y'all got to go. Supper's got to be cooked. These dry, twisted-up sheets got to be pressed and folded."

That night Derrick was so tired from all the dancing he fell asleep blowing the harmonica.

One day Uncle Booker T. and Derrick joined a marching band.
They stopped in front of a white frame house at the edge of town.
Four barefoot boys came running out. They rattled their aluminum
pie pans, tambourines, and homemade drums.

Bang! Bang! Bong! Bong! Ching! Chang! Zing! Zang!

Tall Jimmy, skinny Larry, and the twins, Kevin and Ken, kept time
with the beat. Aunt Fannie Mae trailed behind them, holding baby
LaToya on her left hip and a picnic basket over her right arm.

The boys shouted, "We've been waiting on you! What we going
to play?"

Uncle Booker T. said, "Just play what you feel."

The marching band never skipped a beat until they
reached the neighborhood park. That's where the music
stopped and the play began. Derrick imagined running up and
down the slide like moving his fingers across the harmonica.
Sometimes fast and sometimes slow. The boys ran and never
walked. Laughing, whooping, and yelling, they never talked.

After lunchtime, Uncle Booker T. started playing
a marching song. The boys picked up their instruments.
They marched double quick, turning somersaults, and
hippity-hopping all the way home. Derrick led the way.
Bang! Bang! Bong! Bong! Ching! Chang! Zing! Zang!

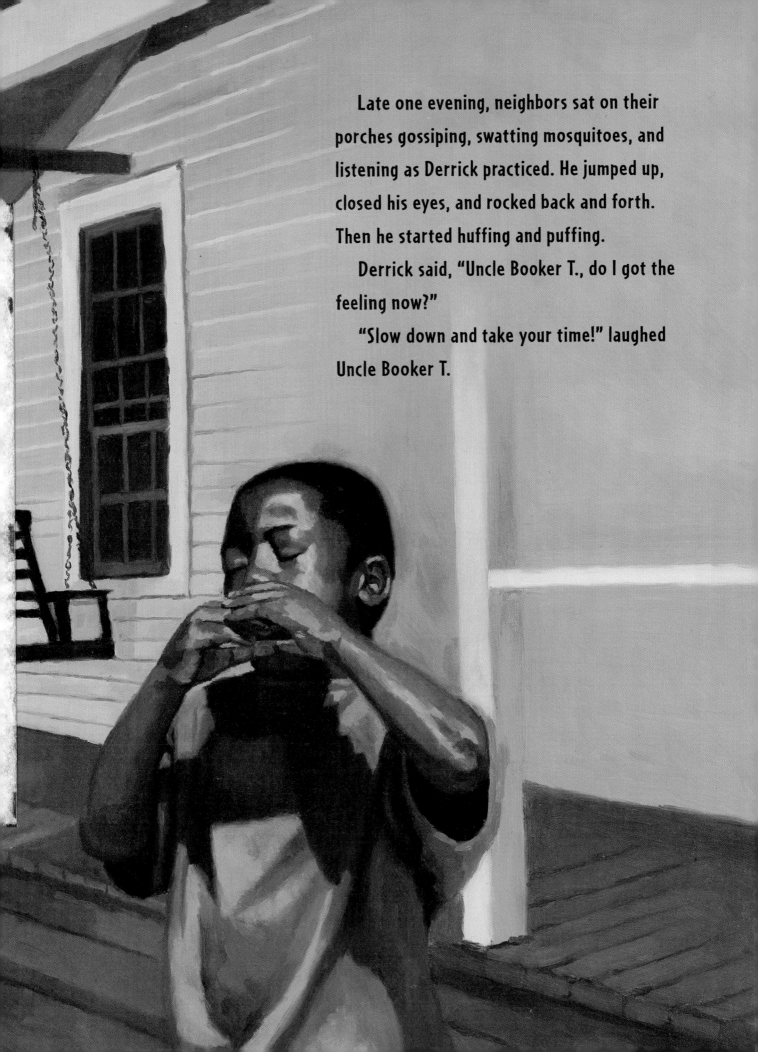

Late one evening, neighbors sat on their porches gossiping, swatting mosquitoes, and listening as Derrick practiced. He jumped up, closed his eyes, and rocked back and forth. Then he started huffing and puffing.

Derrick said, "Uncle Booker T., do I got the feeling now?"

"Slow down and take your time!" laughed Uncle Booker T.

All summer, Derrick slept and ate with the harmonica. He didn't take a break until the morning a cool breeze sent the leaves flying around him. Derrick waited and waited. Uncle Booker T. never came. Derrick found Uncle Booker T. on his front porch, a wool sweater on his thin body.

"Uncle Booker T., why didn't you come?" called Derrick. "You forgot to pick up your harmonica."

"Son, old Arthur came to my door early this morning. He's all in my hands. No music today," moaned Uncle Booker T.

"Who old Arthur?" asked Derrick.

"Your mama ain't told you about arthritis? I'm paining and aching," said Uncle Booker T.

Derrick looked down at Uncle Booker T.'s knotted and bent fingers. Suddenly Derrick knew what would make Uncle Booker T. happy.

Derrick pulled the harmonica out of his pocket. With a deep breath, he started playing notes. Ever so quietly, ever so slowly. Then fast and faster. There were no words, just sweet, sweet music. Derrick rocked back and forth as his hands scooted across the harmonica, breathing new life into the metal.

When the song ended, Derrick opened his eyes and grinned. His hands were wet with sweat. Uncle Booker T. wiped tears from his eyes. He stood up and said, "All right! Yes, indeed! Yes, indeed!"

He hugged Derrick. Derrick didn't say a word. He knew.

"Derrick, this harmonica is yours," said Uncle Booker T. "It will never be just mine anymore. Sometimes you got to pass along the things you love. Keep this old harmonica alive when I'm gone."

Uncle Booker T. and Derrick scampered away, away, away. Cheek to cheek. Face to face. Their noses testing the air. Twisting and turning. Turning and twisting. And though they'd traveled through the dusty streets many times before, it didn't seem the same today. For now, nighttime was hours away and the day had a lot more music left in it.

To Ozie Battle, Dr. John and Mary Moore,
and Jeannie Pamplin, for your support.
– G. B. L.

To my son, Aaquil, to Mr. James Clarke,
and to Lafayette Wood.
– C. B.

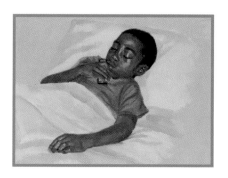

A version of this story was first published in CRICKET: THE MAGAZINE FOR CHILDREN

Text copyright © 2000 by Gwendolyn Battle-Lavert

Illustrations copyright © 2000 by Colin Bootman

Printed in the United States of America

All Rights Reserved

First Edition

The text typeface is Cafeteria Bold.

The artist used oils on illustration board to create the illustrations.

LIBRARY OF CONGRESS CATALOGING-IN-PUBLICATION DATA

Battle-Lavert, Gwendolyn.
The music in Derrick's heart / by Gwendolyn Battle-Lavert;
illustrated by Colin Bootman.–1st ed.
p. cm.
Summary: Uncle Booker T., who makes magic by playing his harmonica
music from his heart, spends the summer teaching Derrick how to play.
ISBN 0-8234-1353-5 (hardcover)
[1. Harmonica–Fiction. 2. Musicians–Fiction. 3. Afro-Americans–
Fiction.] I. Bootman, Colin, ill. II. Title.
PZ7.B32446Mu 2000
[E]–dc21 97-34115
CIP AC

E
BAT

Battle-Lavert,
Gwendolyn.

The music in
Derrick's heart.

33910010883917
$16.95 Grades 1-2 07/28/2000

DATE			

10/17